This book belongs to_____

Home address_____

Date_____

Home Sweet Home

A Homeowner's Journal
and Project Planner

Illustrated by
Mary Engelbreit

Andrews and McMeel
A Universal Press Syndicate Company
Kansas City

is a registered trademark of Mary Engelbreit Enterprises, Inc.

10 9 8 7 6 5 4 3 2

ISBN: 0-8362-4629-2

Text by Patrick Regan
Design by Stephanie Raaf

Home Sweet Home

A Homeowner's Journal
and Project Planner

Contents

Contents

How to Use This Book

ave you ever had to run back to the store for another gallon of paint halfway through painting your living room? Or frantically fish through your pockets for the window measurements you jotted down on a piece of scrap paper? Does the thought of finding a two-week old hardware store receipt send you into a state of panic?

If you can answer "yes" to any of these questions, you must be a homeowner! And if you own a home, you've surely said to yourself, "I wish there was *one* place I could keep everything I know and need to know about my house." This book can be that place.

Whether you've just purchased your home or have lived in it for 20 years, the *Homeowner's Journal and Project Planner* will help you to be more organized and efficient (and *sane*) in the day-to-day challenge of maintaining and improving your home.

In the first section of this book, you'll find a place to record helpful home-related phone numbers and addresses, a page to record a brief history of your home, and several blank pages to which you can affix photos of your home improvement projects as they move toward completion. On the Project Planner pages, you can describe, prioritize, budget, and track specific projects that you plan to tackle in the future.

A room-by-room journal begins on page 25. In this section, four pages are provided for each main room of a typical home. Here, you can write down your goals and priorities for the room and record all the pertinent details regarding the room's dimensions, window treatments, and floor, ceiling, and wall coverings. Grid lines are also provided for keeping notes or miscellaneous room layouts. Remember, every home is different, so if certain sections of this book don't apply to your home, leave them blank or use the space for more appropriate records.

The Decorating Ideas section includes furniture templates and several grid-lined pages for your room-decorating notes and sketches. Two pockets inside the back cover provide handy storage for receipts and for decorating ideas copied from books or clipped from magazines.

Beginning on page 119 is a section for recording information about the exterior of your home, your garage, deck, patio, and other outdoor areas and structures. Following that are several pages on which you can record warranty and service information for all of your home's major appliances. And lastly, the Reference section at the end of this journal contains tips for painting and wallpapering and other helpful information.

On every trip to the decorating center or hardware store, make this book your constant companion. Make it the "one place" for your household information, plans, records, and receipts, and you'll be amazed how organized and efficient home ownership can be.

Helpful Names & Numbers

Buyer's Real Estate Agent

Company_____

Contact_____

Phone_____

Address_____

_____

Seller's Real Estate Agent

Company_____

Contact_____

Phone_____

Address_____

_____

Builder

Company_____

Contact_____

Phone_____

Address_____

_____

Mortgage

Company_____

Contact_____

Phone_____

Address_____

_____

Title

Company_____

Contact_____

Phone_____

Address_____

_____

Insurance

Company_____

Contact_____

Phone_____

Address_____

_____

Mechanical/Structural Inspector

Company_____

Contact_____

Phone_____

Address_____

_____

Exterminator

Company_____

Contact_____

Phone_____

Address_____

_____

Plumber

Company_____

Contact_____

Phone_____

Address_____

_____

Electrician

Company_____

Contact_____

Phone_____

Address_____

_____

HVAC Repair

    Company_____

    Contact_____

    Phone_____

    Address_____

_____

Painter

    Company_____

    Contact_____

    Phone_____

    Address_____

_____

Lawn Maintenance

    Company_____

    Contact_____

    Phone_____

    Address_____

_____

Neighbor

    Name_____

    Phone_____

    Address_____

_____

_____

Neighbor

    Name_____

    Phone_____

    Address_____

_____

_____

Decorator

    Company_____

    Contact_____

    Phone_____

    Address_____

_____

Wallpaper Hanger

    Company_____

    Contact_____

    Phone_____

    Address_____

_____

Neighborhood Association

    Company_____

    Contact_____

    Phone_____

    Address_____

_____

Neighbor

    Name_____

    Phone_____

    Address_____

_____

_____

Neighbor

    Name_____

    Phone_____

    Address_____

_____

_____

Other Names & Numbers

Company_____

    Contact _____

    Phone_____

    Address _____

_____

_____

Company_____

    Contact _____

    Phone_____

    Address _____

_____

_____

Company_____

    Contact _____

    Phone_____

    Address _____

_____

_____

Company_____

    Contact _____

    Phone_____

    Address _____

_____

_____

Company_____

    Contact _____

    Phone_____

    Address _____

_____

_____

Company_____

    Contact _____

    Phone_____

    Address _____

_____

_____

Company_____

    Contact _____

    Phone_____

    Address _____

_____

_____

Company_____

    Contact _____

    Phone_____

    Address _____

_____

_____

Company_____

    Contact _____

    Phone_____

    Address _____

_____

_____

Company_____

    Contact _____

    Phone_____

    Address _____

_____

_____

Company _____   Company _____

   Contact _____   Contact _____

   Phone _____   Phone _____

   Address _____   Address _____

_____   _____

_____   _____

Company _____   Company _____

   Contact _____   Contact _____

   Phone _____   Phone _____

   Address _____   Address _____

_____   _____

_____   _____

Company _____   Company _____

   Contact _____   Contact _____

   Phone _____   Phone _____

   Address _____   Address _____

_____   _____

_____   _____

Company _____   Company _____

   Contact _____   Contact _____

   Phone _____   Phone _____

   Address _____   Address _____

_____   _____

_____   _____

Company _____   Company _____

   Contact _____   Contact _____

   Phone _____   Phone _____

   Address _____   Address _____

_____   _____

_____   _____

HOME IS WHERE THE HEART IS

History of Our Home

Date built _____

Built by _____

_____

Price of home when built _____

Our purchase price _____

Appraised value _____

Purchase date _____

Closing date _____

Move-in date _____

Real estate agent _____

Mortgage company _____

   Contact _____

Interest rate and type _____

_____

Points _____

Terms _____

Total square footage _____

Notes _____

_____

_____

_____

_____

_____

_____

_____

_____

_____

(Include the home's sales sheet if available in the pocket provided at the back of the book.)

Project Planner

Use these pages to plan various household projects and to track their progress to completion. Use the grids to describe and prioritize each of your projects and to sketch out diagrams and designs.

Project
Estimated budget
Time frame
Description

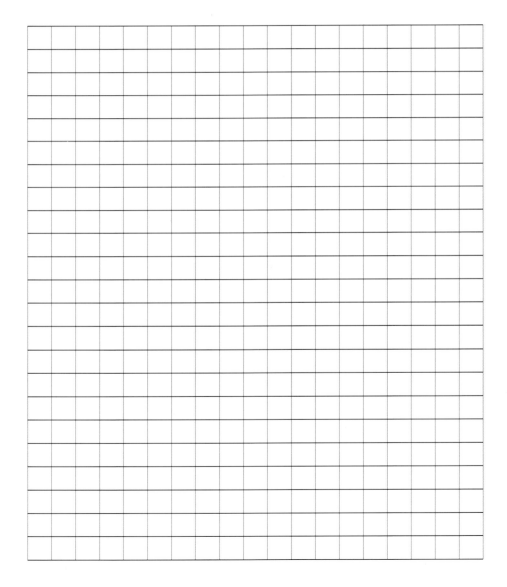

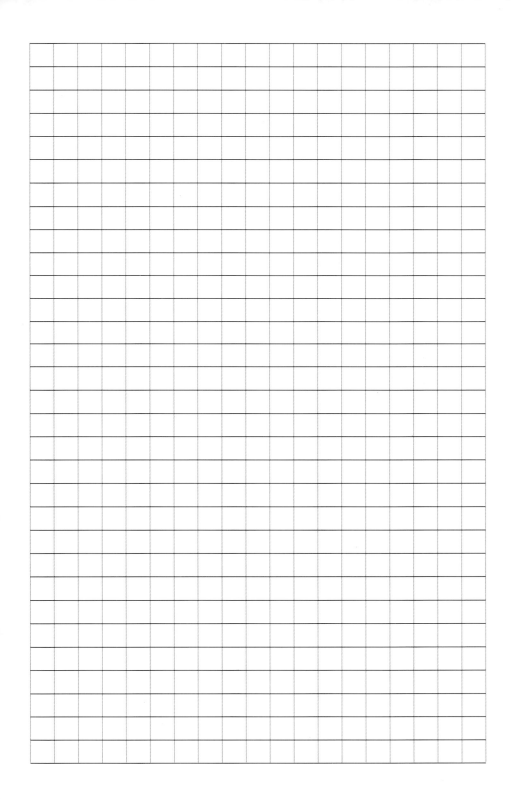

Project
Planner

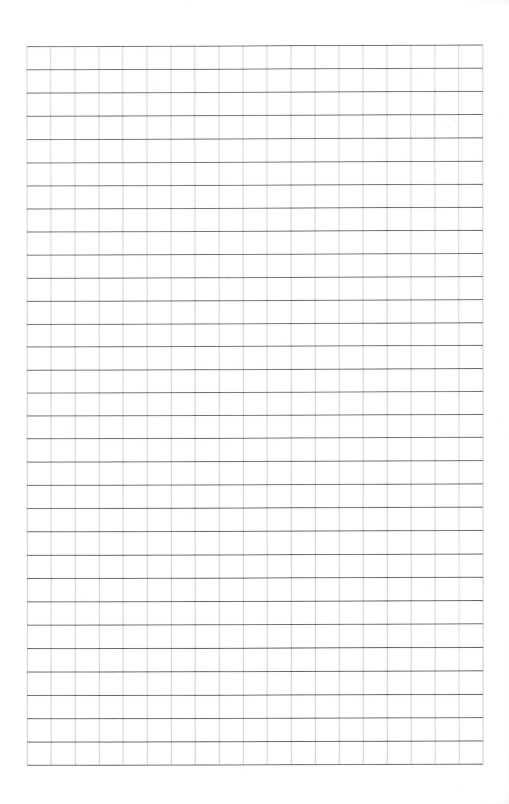

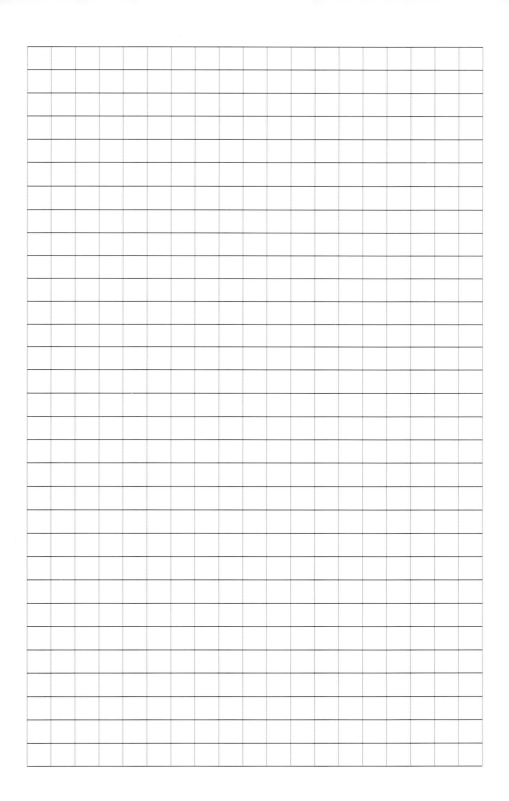

Photos

On this and the following three pages, attach photos of your home as it was when you first moved in. Also include photos of home improvement projects in progress and as they are completed.

Photos

EVERYONE NEEDS THEIR OWN SPOT.

· ROBERT WHALEN ·

Room-by-Room Journal
and
Decorating Ideas

Front Entry Way

Room Dimensions _____ x _____ x _____

Goals and priorities for this room_____

_____

_____

_____

_____

_____

_____

_____

_____

_____

Floor

Type of floor (hardwood, tile, concrete, etc.)_____

_____

Type of floor covering_____

_____

Coverage area (sq. ft.)_____

Purchased from _____

_____

Cost per unit/Total cost_____

Installed by_____

    Date_____

Pattern, color, brand, number_____

_____

Cleaning instructions_____

_____

Notes_____

_____

_____

Walls

Coverage area (sq. ft.)_____

Type of covering_____

_____

Purchased from _____

_____

Cost per unit/Total cost_____

Applied by_____

    Date_____

Pattern, color, brand, number_____

_____

Trim/woodwork_____

_____

Notes_____

_____

_____

Front
Entry Way

Ceiling

Coverage area (sq. ft.)_____

Type of ceiling_____

Type of covering_____

Purchased from_____

_____

Cost per unit/Total cost_____

Applied by_____

Date_____

Pattern, color, brand, number_____

_____

Notes_____

_____

_____

Window Treatments

Type of treatments_____

_____

Purchased from_____

_____

Window dimensions (see diagram, page 134)_____

_____

_____

Size of treatments_____

_____

Cleaning instructions_____

_____

_____

Notes_____

_____

_____

Miscellaneous Notes or Layouts

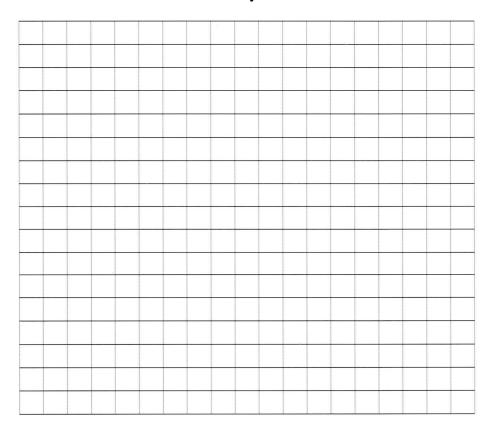

Attach swatches, paint chips, carpet yarns,
or other samples here.

Living Room

Room Dimensions _____ x _____ x _____

Goals and priorities for this room_____

_____

_____

_____

_____

_____

_____

_____

_____

_____

_____

_____

Floor

Type of floor (hardwood, tile, concrete, etc.)_____

_____

Type of floor covering_____

_____

Coverage area (sq. ft.)_____

Purchased from_____

_____

Cost per unit/Total cost_____

Installed by_____

Date_____

Pattern, color, brand, number_____

_____

Cleaning instructions_____

_____

Notes_____

_____

_____

Walls

Coverage area (sq. ft.)_____

Type of covering_____

_____

Purchased from _____

_____

Cost per unit/Total cost_____

Applied by_____

    Date_____

Pattern, color, brand, number_____

_____

Trim/woodwork_____

_____

Notes_____

_____

_____

Living Room

Ceiling

Coverage area (sq. ft.)_____

Type of ceiling_____

Type of covering_____

Purchased from_____

_____

Cost per unit/Total cost_____

Applied by_____

    Date_____

Pattern, color, brand, number_____

_____

Notes_____

_____

_____

Window Treatments

Type of treatments_____

_____

Purchased from_____

_____

Window dimensions (see diagram, page 134)_____

_____

_____

Size of treatments_____

_____

Cleaning instructions_____

_____

_____

Notes_____

_____

_____

Miscellaneous Notes or Layouts

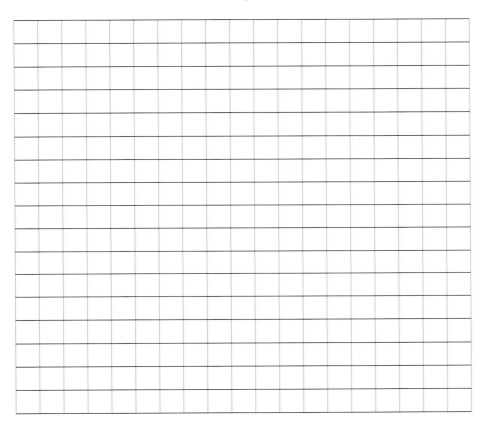

Attach swatches, paint chips, carpet yarns,
or other samples here.

Dining Room

Room Dimensions ———— x ———— x ————

Goals and priorities for this room ————————————
———————————————————————————
———————————————————————————
———————————————————————————
———————————————————————————
———————————————————————————
———————————————————————————
———————————————————————————
———————————————————————————
———————————————————————————

Floor

Type of floor (hardwood, tile, concrete, etc.) ————————
———————————————————————————

Type of floor covering ————————————————————
———————————————————————————

Coverage area (sq. ft.) ————————————————————
Purchased from ——————————————————————
———————————————————————————

Cost per unit/Total cost ——————————————————
Installed by ————————————————————————
      Date ——————————————————————————
Pattern, color, brand, number ————————————————
———————————————————————————

Cleaning instructions ————————————————————
———————————————————————————

Notes ——————————————————————————
———————————————————————————
———————————————————————————

Walls

Coverage area (sq. ft.)_____

Type of covering_____

_____

Purchased from _____

_____

Cost per unit/Total cost_____

Applied by_____

    Date_____

Pattern, color, brand, number_____

_____

Trim/woodwork_____

_____

Notes_____

_____

_____

Dining Room

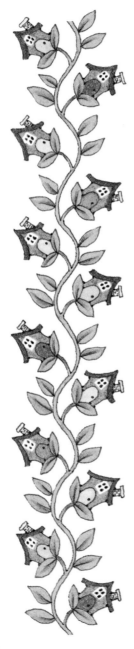

Ceiling

Coverage area (sq. ft.)_____

Type of ceiling_____

Type of covering_____

Purchased from_____

_____

Cost per unit/Total cost_____

Applied by_____

   Date_____

Pattern, color, brand, number_____

_____

Notes_____

_____

_____

Window Treatments

Type of treatments_____

_____

Purchased from_____

_____

Window dimensions (see diagram, page 134)_____

_____

_____

Size of treatments_____

_____

Cleaning instructions_____

_____

_____

Notes_____

_____

_____

Miscellaneous Notes or Layouts

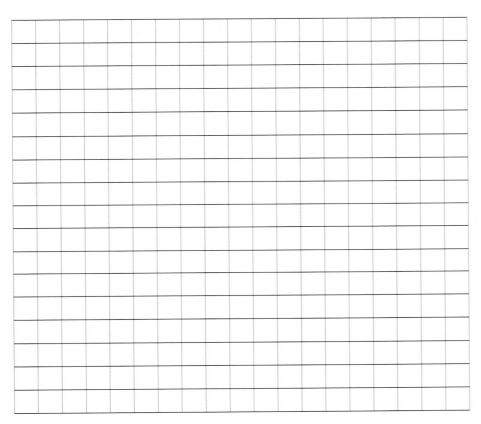

Attach swatches, paint chips, carpet yarns,
or other samples here.

Family Room

Room Dimensions _____ x _____ x _____

Goals and priorities for this room_____

_____

_____

_____

_____

_____

_____

_____

_____

_____

Floor

Type of floor (hardwood, tile, concrete, etc.)_____

_____

Type of floor covering_____

_____

Coverage area (sq. ft.)_____

Purchased from_____

_____

Cost per unit/Total cost_____

Installed by_____

    Date_____

Pattern, color, brand, number_____

_____

Cleaning instructions_____

_____

Notes_____

_____

_____

Walls

Coverage area (sq. ft.)_____

Type of covering_____

_____

Purchased from _____

_____

Cost per unit/Total cost_____

Applied by_____

    Date_____

Pattern, color, brand, number_____

_____

Trim/woodwork_____

_____

Notes_____

_____

_____

Family Room

Ceiling

Coverage area (sq. ft.)_____

Type of ceiling_____

Type of covering_____

Purchased from_____

_____

Cost per unit/Total cost_____

Applied by_____

Date_____

Pattern, color, brand, number_____

_____

Notes_____

_____

_____

Window Treatments

Type of treatments_____

_____

Purchased from_____

_____

Window dimensions (see diagram, page 134)_____

_____

_____

Size of treatments_____

_____

Cleaning instructions_____

_____

_____

Notes_____

_____

_____

Miscellaneous Notes or Layouts

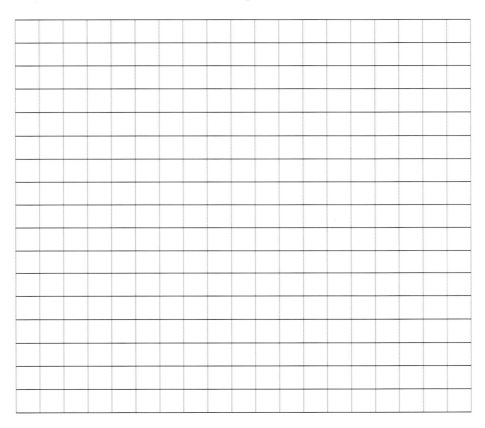

Attach swatches, paint chips, carpet yarns,
or other samples here.

Office/Den

Room Dimensions _____ x _____ x _____

Goals and priorities for this room_____

_____

_____

_____

_____

_____

_____

_____

_____

_____

_____

Floor

Type of floor (hardwood, tile, concrete, etc.)_____

_____

Type of floor covering_____

_____

Coverage area (sq. ft.)_____

Purchased from _____

_____

Cost per unit/Total cost_____

Installed by_____

     Date_____

Pattern, color, brand, number_____

_____

Cleaning instructions_____

_____

Notes_____

_____

_____

Walls

Coverage area (sq. ft.)_____

Type of covering_____

_____

Purchased from _____

_____

Cost per unit/Total cost_____

Applied by_____

   Date_____

Pattern, color, brand, number_____

_____

Trim/woodwork_____

_____

Notes_____

_____

_____

Office/Den

Ceiling

Coverage area (sq. ft.)_____

Type of ceiling_____

Type of covering_____

Purchased from_____

_____

Cost per unit/Total cost_____

Applied by_____

    Date_____

Pattern, color, brand, number_____

_____

Notes_____

_____

_____

Window Treatments

Type of treatments_____

_____

Purchased from_____

_____

Window dimensions (see diagram, page 134)_____

_____

_____

Size of treatments_____

_____

Cleaning instructions_____

_____

_____

Notes_____

_____

_____

Miscellaneous Notes or Layouts

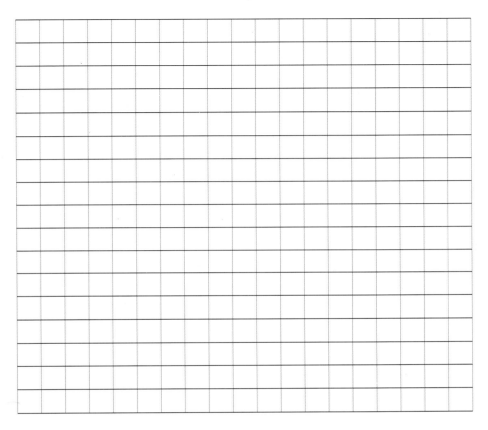

Attach swatches, paint chips, carpet yarns,
or other samples here.

Kitchen

Room Dimensions ———— x ———— x ————

Goals and priorities for this room _____

_____

_____

_____

_____

_____

_____

_____

_____

_____

_____

Floor

Type of floor (hardwood, tile, concrete, etc.) _____

_____

Type of floor covering _____

_____

Coverage area (sq. ft.) _____

Purchased from _____

_____

Cost per unit/Total cost _____

Installed by _____

   Date _____

Pattern, color, brand, number _____

_____

Cleaning instructions _____

_____

Notes _____

_____

_____

Walls

Coverage area (sq. ft.)_____

Type of covering_____

_____

Purchased from _____

_____

Cost per unit/Total cost_____

Applied by_____

     Date_____

Pattern, color, brand, number_____

_____

Trim/woodwork_____

_____

Notes_____

_____

_____

Kitchen

Ceiling

Coverage area (sq. ft.)_____

Type of ceiling_____

Type of covering_____

Purchased from_____

_____

Cost per unit/Total cost_____

Applied by_____

    Date_____

Pattern, color, brand, number_____

_____

Notes_____

_____

_____

Window Treatments

Type of treatments_____

_____

Purchased from _____

_____

Window dimensions (see diagram, page 134)_____

_____

_____

Size of treatments_____

_____

Cleaning instructions_____

_____

_____

Notes_____

_____

_____

Cabinets and Countertops

Purchased from _____

_____

Installed by _____

    Date _____

Cabinet material (type of wood) _____

    Type of finish (paint, stain, etc.) _____

    Pattern, color, brand, number _____

Countertop material (Formica, laminate, etc.) _____

    Pattern, color, brand, number _____

Notes _____

_____

Miscellaneous Notes, Layouts or Samples

Note: Record information about appliances on pages 130-133.

Mudroom

Room Dimensions _____ x _____ x _____

Goals and priorities for this room_____

_____

_____

_____

_____

_____

_____

_____

_____

_____

_____

_____

Floor

Type of floor (hardwood, tile, concrete, etc.)_____

_____

Type of floor covering_____

_____

Coverage area (sq. ft.)_____

Purchased from_____

_____

Cost per unit/Total cost_____

Installed by_____

Date_____

Pattern, color, brand, number_____

_____

Cleaning instructions_____

_____

Notes_____

_____

_____

Walls

Coverage area (sq. ft.)_____

Type of covering_____

_____

Purchased from _____

_____

Cost per unit/Total cost_____

Applied by_____

     Date_____

Pattern, color, brand, number_____

_____

Trim/woodwork_____

_____

Notes_____

_____

_____

Mudroom

Ceiling

Coverage area (sq. ft.)_____

Type of ceiling_____

Type of covering_____

Purchased from_____

_____

Cost per unit/Total cost_____

Applied by_____

　　　Date_____

Pattern, color, brand, number_____

Notes_____

_____

_____

Window Treatments

Type of treatments_____

_____

Purchased from_____

_____

Window dimensions (see diagram, page 134)_____

_____

_____

Size of treatments_____

_____

Cleaning instructions_____

_____

_____

Notes_____

_____

_____

_____

Miscellaneous Notes or Layouts

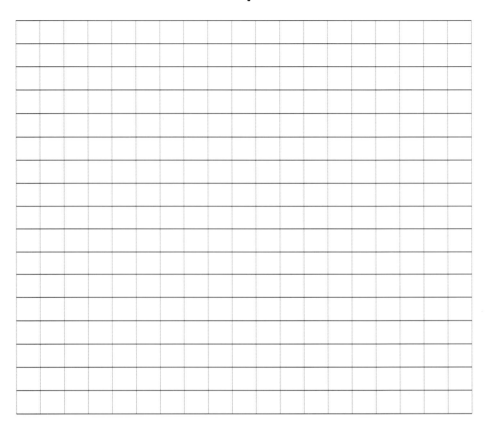

Attach swatches, paint chips, carpet yarns,
or other samples here.

Stairway

Room Dimensions _____ x _____ x _____

Goals and priorities for this room_____

_____

_____

_____

_____

_____

_____

_____

_____

_____

Floor

Type of floor (hardwood, tile, concrete, etc.)_____

_____

Type of floor covering_____

_____

Coverage area (sq. ft.)_____

Purchased from_____

_____

Cost per unit/Total cost_____

Installed by_____

    Date_____

Pattern, color, brand, number_____

_____

Cleaning instructions_____

_____

Notes_____

_____

_____

Walls

Coverage area (sq. ft.)_____

Type of covering_____

_____

Purchased from _____

_____

Cost per unit/Total cost_____

Applied by_____

    Date_____

Pattern, color, brand, number_____

_____

Trim/woodwork_____

_____

Notes_____

_____

_____

Stairway

Ceiling

Coverage area (sq. ft.)_____

Type of ceiling_____

Type of covering_____

Purchased from_____

_____

Cost per unit/Total cost_____

Applied by_____

Date_____

Pattern, color, brand, number_____

_____

Notes_____

_____

_____

Window Treatments

Type of treatments_____

_____

Purchased from_____

_____

Window dimensions (see diagram, page 134)_____

_____

_____

Size of treatments_____

_____

Cleaning instructions_____

_____

_____

Notes_____

_____

_____

Miscellaneous Notes or Layouts

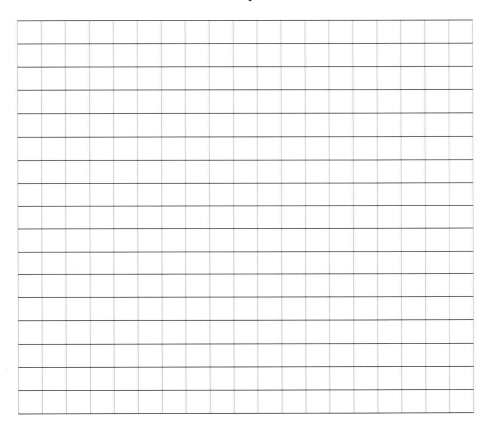

Attach swatches, paint chips, carpet yarns,
or other samples here.

Hallway

Room Dimensions ———— x ———— x ————

Goals and priorities for this room _____

_____

_____

_____

_____

_____

_____

_____

_____

_____

Floor

Type of floor (hardwood, tile, concrete, etc.) _____

_____

Type of floor covering _____

_____

Coverage area (sq. ft.) _____

Purchased from _____

_____

Cost per unit/Total cost _____

Installed by _____

       Date _____

Pattern, color, brand, number _____

_____

Cleaning instructions _____

_____

Notes _____

_____

_____

Walls

Coverage area (sq. ft.)_____

Type of covering_____

_____

Purchased from _____

_____

Cost per unit/Total cost_____

Applied by_____

    Date_____

Pattern, color, brand, number_____

_____

Trim/woodwork_____

_____

Notes_____

_____

_____

Hallway

Ceiling

Coverage area (sq. ft.)_____

Type of ceiling_____

Type of covering_____

Purchased from_____

_____

Cost per unit/Total cost_____

Applied by_____

Date_____

Pattern, color, brand, number_____

_____

Notes_____

_____

_____

Window Treatments

Type of treatments_____

_____

Purchased from_____

_____

Window dimensions (see diagram, page 134)_____

_____

_____

Size of treatments_____

_____

Cleaning instructions_____

_____

_____

Notes_____

_____

_____

Miscellaneous Notes or Layouts

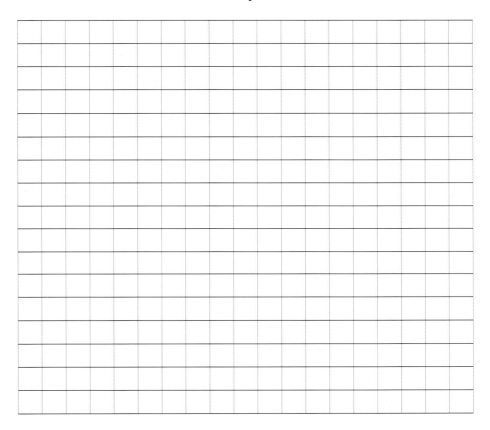

Attach swatches, paint chips, carpet yarns,
or other samples here.

Master Bedroom

Room Dimensions ———— x ———— x ————

Goals and priorities for this room _____

_____

_____

_____

_____

_____

_____

_____

_____

_____

_____

_____

Floor

Type of floor (hardwood, tile, concrete, etc.) _____

_____

Type of floor covering _____

_____

Coverage area (sq. ft.) _____

Purchased from _____

_____

Cost per unit/Total cost _____

Installed by _____

    Date _____

Pattern, color, brand, number _____

_____

Cleaning instructions _____

_____

Notes _____

_____

_____

Walls

Coverage area (sq. ft.)_____

Type of covering_____

_____

Purchased from _____

_____

Cost per unit/Total cost_____

Applied by_____

Date_____

Pattern, color, brand, number_____

_____

Trim/woodwork_____

_____

Notes_____

_____

_____

Master Bedroom

Ceiling

Coverage area (sq. ft.)_____

Type of ceiling_____

Type of covering_____

Purchased from_____

_____

Cost per unit/Total cost_____

Applied by_____

  Date_____

Pattern, color, brand, number_____

Notes_____

_____

_____

Window Treatments

Type of treatments_____

_____

Purchased from_____

_____

Window dimensions (see diagram, page 134)_____

_____

_____

Size of treatments_____

_____

Cleaning instructions_____

_____

_____

Notes_____

_____

_____

Miscellaneous Notes or Layouts

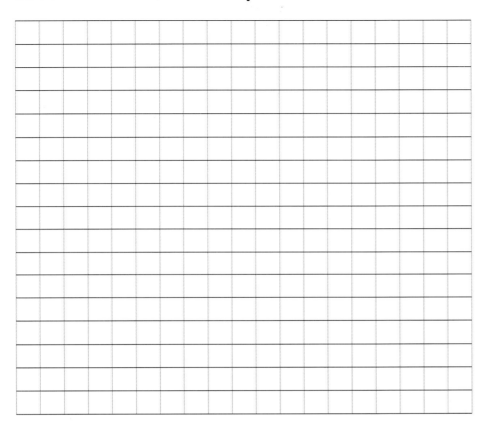

Attach swatches, paint chips, carpet yarns,
or other samples here.

Bedroom Two

Room Dimensions _____ x _____ x _____

Goals and priorities for this room_____

_____

_____

_____

_____

_____

_____

_____

_____

_____

_____

Floor

Type of floor (hardwood, tile, concrete, etc.)_____

_____

Type of floor covering_____

_____

Coverage area (sq. ft.)_____

Purchased from _____

_____

Cost per unit/Total cost_____

Installed by_____

    Date_____

Pattern, color, brand, number_____

_____

Cleaning instructions_____

_____

Notes_____

_____

_____

Walls

Coverage area (sq. ft.)_____

Type of covering_____

_____

Purchased from _____

_____

Cost per unit/Total cost_____

Applied by_____

   Date_____

Pattern, color, brand, number_____

_____

Trim/woodwork_____

_____

Notes_____

_____

_____

I WANT TO LIVE
BY THE SIDE OF
·THE ROAD·
AND BE A FRIEND
·TO MAN·

CEASE TO ASK WHAT THE MORROW WILL BRING
AND SET DOWN AS GAIN EACH DAY THAT FORTUNE GRANTS

Bedroom Two

Ceiling

Coverage area (sq. ft.)_____

Type of ceiling_____

Type of covering_____

Purchased from_____

_____

Cost per unit/Total cost_____

Applied by_____

   Date_____

Pattern, color, brand, number_____

_____

Notes_____

_____

_____

Window Treatments

Type of treatments_____

_____

Purchased from_____

_____

Window dimensions (see diagram, page 134)_____

_____

_____

Size of treatments_____

_____

Cleaning instructions_____

_____

_____

Notes_____

_____

_____

Miscellaneous Notes or Layouts

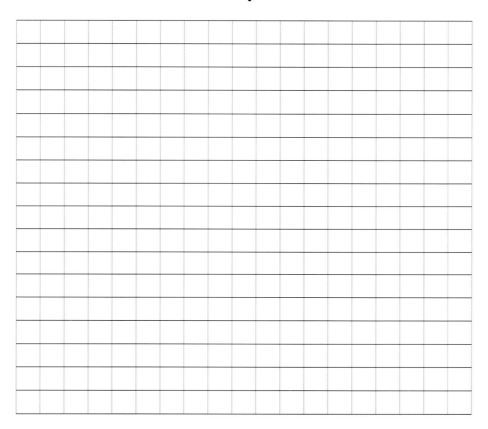

Attach swatches, paint chips, carpet yarns,
or other samples here.

Bedroom Three

Room Dimensions ———— x ———— x ————

Goals and priorities for this room —————————————————
_____
_____
_____
_____
_____
_____
_____
_____
_____
_____

Floor

Type of floor (hardwood, tile, concrete, etc.) ——————————
_____

Type of floor covering ————————————————————
_____

Coverage area (sq. ft.) ——————————————————————

Purchased from ———————————————————————
_____

Cost per unit/Total cost ———————————————————

Installed by ——————————————————————————

    Date ————————————————————————————

Pattern, color, brand, number ————————————————
_____

Cleaning instructions ————————————————————
_____

Notes ——————————————————————————————
_____
_____

Walls

Coverage area (sq. ft.)_____

Type of covering_____

_____

Purchased from _____

_____

Cost per unit/Total cost_____

Applied by_____

    Date_____

Pattern, color, brand, number_____

_____

Trim/woodwork_____

_____

Notes_____

_____

Bedroom Three

Ceiling

Coverage area (sq. ft.)_____

Type of ceiling_____

Type of covering_____

Purchased from _____

_____

Cost per unit/Total cost_____

Applied by_____

    Date_____

Pattern, color, brand, number_____

_____

Notes_____

_____

_____

Window Treatments

Type of treatments_____

_____

Purchased from _____

_____

Window dimensions (see diagram, page 134)_____

_____

_____

Size of treatments_____

_____

Cleaning instructions_____

_____

_____

Notes_____

_____

_____

Miscellaneous Notes or Layouts

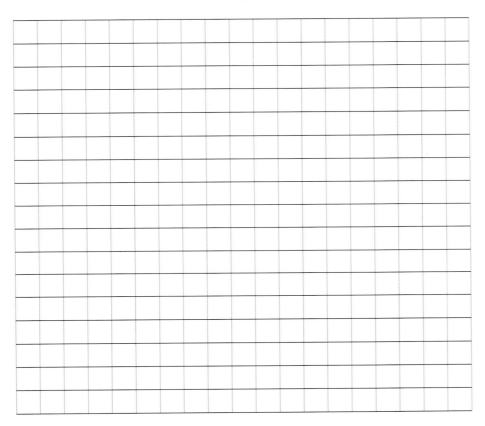

Attach swatches, paint chips, carpet yarns,
or other samples here.

Bedroom Four

Room Dimensions _____ x _____ x _____

Goals and priorities for this room_____

_____

_____

_____

_____

_____

_____

_____

_____

_____

_____

Floor

Type of floor (hardwood, tile, concrete, etc.)_____

_____

Type of floor covering_____

_____

Coverage area (sq. ft.)_____

Purchased from _____

_____

Cost per unit/Total cost_____

Installed by_____

     Date_____

Pattern, color, brand, number_____

_____

Cleaning instructions_____

_____

Notes_____

_____

_____

Walls

Coverage area (sq. ft.)_____

Type of covering_____

_____

Purchased from _____

_____

Cost per unit/Total cost_____

Applied by_____

    Date_____

Pattern, color, brand, number_____

_____

Trim/woodwork_____

_____

Notes_____

_____

_____

Bedroom Four

Ceiling

Coverage area (sq. ft.)_____

Type of ceiling_____

Type of covering_____

Purchased from _____

_____

Cost per unit/Total cost_____

Applied by_____

    Date_____

Pattern, color, brand, number_____

_____

Notes_____

_____

_____

Window Treatments

Type of treatments_____

_____

Purchased from _____

_____

Window dimensions (see diagram, page 134)_____

_____

Size of treatments_____

_____

Cleaning instructions_____

_____

_____

Notes_____

_____

_____

Miscellaneous Notes or Layouts

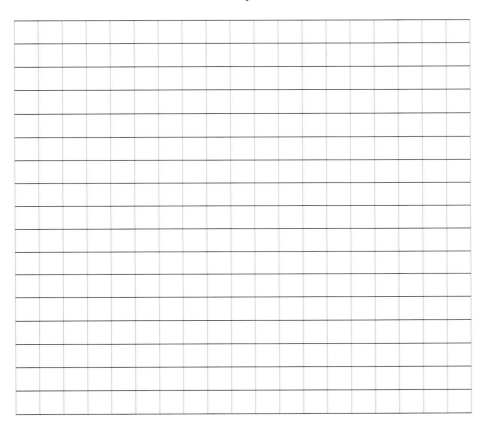

Attach swatches, paint chips, carpet yarns,
or other samples here.

Master Bathroom

Room Dimensions _____ x _____ x _____

Goals and priorities for this room_____

_____

_____

_____

_____

_____

_____

_____

_____

_____

Floor

Type of floor (hardwood, tile, concrete, etc.)_____

_____

Type of floor covering_____

_____

Coverage area (sq. ft.)_____

Purchased from_____

_____

Cost per unit/Total cost_____

Installed by_____

　　Date_____

Pattern, color, brand, number_____

_____

Cleaning instructions_____

_____

Notes_____

_____

_____

Walls

Coverage area (sq. ft.)_____

Type of covering_____

_____

Purchased from _____

_____

Cost per unit/Total cost_____

Applied by_____

    Date_____

Pattern, color, brand, number_____

_____

Trim/woodwork_____

_____

Notes_____

_____

_____

Master Bathroom

Ceiling

Coverage area (sq. ft.)_____

Type of ceiling_____

Type of covering_____

Purchased from _____

_____

Cost per unit/Total cost_____

Applied by_____

   Date_____

Pattern, color, brand, number_____

_____

Notes_____

_____

_____

Window Treatments

Type of treatments_____

_____

Purchased from _____

_____

Window dimensions (see diagram, page 134)_____

_____

_____

Size of treatments_____

_____

Cleaning instructions_____

_____

_____

Notes_____

_____

_____

Fixtures

Purchased from, date_____

_____

Type, brand, color_____

_____

Notes_____

_____

_____

Miscellaneous Notes, Layouts or Samples

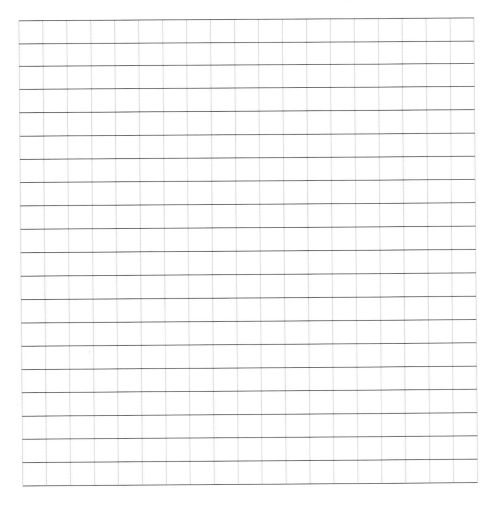

Bathroom Two

Room Dimensions _____ x _____ x _____

Goals and priorities for this room_____

_____

_____

_____

_____

_____

_____

_____

_____

_____

_____

Floor

Type of floor (hardwood, tile, concrete, etc.)_____

_____

Type of floor covering_____

_____

Coverage area (sq. ft.)_____

Purchased from_____

_____

Cost per unit/Total cost_____

Installed by_____

   Date_____

Pattern, color, brand, number_____

_____

Cleaning instructions_____

_____

Notes_____

_____

_____

Walls

Coverage area (sq. ft.)_____

Type of covering_____

_____

Purchased from _____

_____

Cost per unit/Total cost_____

Applied by_____

    Date_____

Pattern, color, brand, number_____

_____

Trim/woodwork_____

_____

Notes_____

_____

_____

Bathroom Two

Ceiling

Coverage area (sq. ft.)_____

Type of ceiling_____

Type of covering_____

Purchased from _____

_____

Cost per unit/Total cost_____

Applied by_____

    Date_____

Pattern, color, brand, number_____

_____

Notes_____

_____

_____

Window Treatments

Type of treatments_____

_____

Purchased from _____

_____

Window dimensions (see diagram, page 134)_____

_____

_____

Size of treatments_____

_____

Cleaning instructions_____

_____

_____

Notes_____

_____

_____

Fixtures

Purchased from, date_____

_____

Type, brand, color_____

_____

Notes_____

_____

_____

Miscellaneous Notes, Layouts or Samples

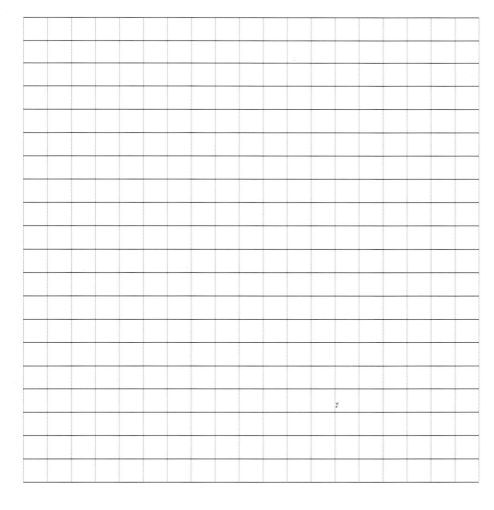

Bathroom
Three

Room Dimensions _____ x _____ x _____

Goals and priorities for this room_____
_____
_____
_____
_____
_____
_____
_____
_____
_____
_____

Floor

Type of floor (hardwood, tile, concrete, etc.)_____
_____

Type of floor covering_____
_____

Coverage area (sq. ft.)_____

Purchased from _____
_____

Cost per unit/Total cost_____

Installed by_____

    Date_____

Pattern, color, brand, number_____
_____

Cleaning instructions_____
_____

Notes_____
_____
_____

Walls

Coverage area (sq. ft.)_____

Type of covering_____

_____

Purchased from _____

_____

Cost per unit/Total cost _____

Applied by_____

    Date_____

Pattern, color, brand, number_____

_____

Trim/woodwork_____

_____

Notes_____

_____

_____

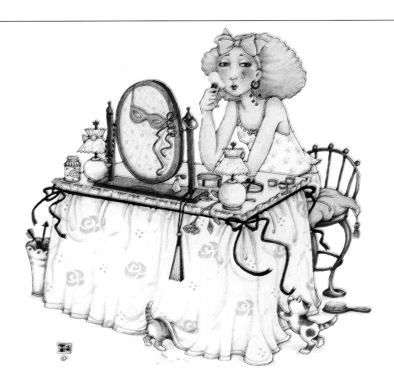

Bathroom Three

Ceiling

Coverage area (sq. ft.)_____

Type of ceiling_____

Type of covering_____

Purchased from _____

_____

Cost per unit/Total cost_____

Applied by_____

Date_____

Pattern, color, brand, number_____

_____

Notes_____

_____

_____

Window Treatments

Type of treatments_____

_____

Purchased from _____

_____

Window dimensions (see diagram, page 134)_____

_____

_____

Size of treatments_____

_____

Cleaning instructions_____

_____

_____

Notes_____

_____

_____

Fixtures

Purchased from, date_____

_____

Type, brand, color_____

_____

Notes_____

_____

_____

Miscellaneous Notes, Layouts or Samples

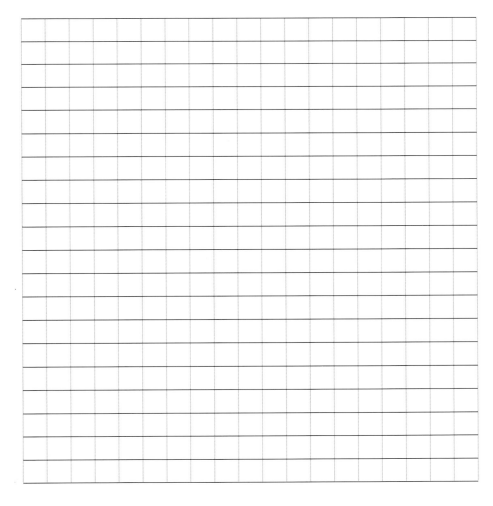

Laundry Room

Room Dimensions _____ x _____ x _____

Goals and priorities for this room_____

_____

_____

_____

_____

_____

_____

_____

_____

_____

_____

Floor

Type of floor (hardwood, tile, concrete, etc.)_____

_____

Type of floor covering_____

_____

Coverage area (sq. ft.)_____

Purchased from _____

_____

Cost per unit/Total cost_____

Installed by_____

    Date_____

Pattern, color, brand, number_____

_____

Cleaning instructions_____

_____

Notes_____

_____

_____

Walls

Coverage area (sq. ft.)_____

Type of covering_____

_____

Purchased from_____

_____

Cost per unit/Total cost_____

Applied by_____

Date_____

Pattern, color, brand, number_____

_____

Trim/woodwork_____

_____

Notes_____

_____

_____

Laundry Room

Ceiling

Coverage area (sq. ft.)_____

Type of ceiling_____

Type of covering_____

Purchased from _____

_____

Cost per unit/Total cost_____

Applied by_____

    Date_____

Pattern, color, brand, number_____

_____

Notes_____

_____

_____

Window Treatments

Type of treatments_____

_____

Purchased from _____

_____

Window dimensions (see diagram, page 134)_____

_____

_____

Size of treatments_____

_____

Cleaning instructions_____

_____

_____

Notes_____

_____

_____

Miscellaneous Notes or Layouts

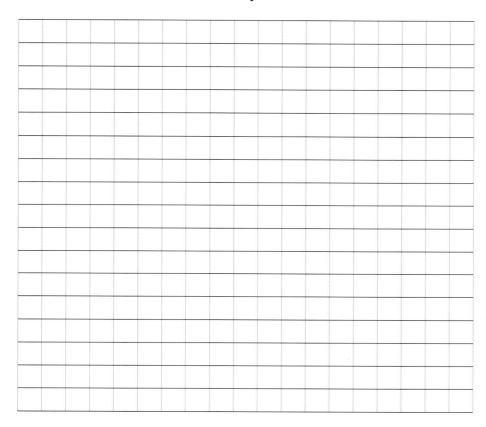

Attach swatches, paint chips, carpet yarns,
or other samples here.

Note: Record information about appliances on pages 130-133.

Attic

Room Dimensions _____ x _____ x _____

Goals and priorities for this room_____

_____

_____

_____

_____

_____

_____

_____

_____

_____

_____

Floor

Type of floor (hardwood, tile, concrete, etc.)_____

_____

Type of floor covering_____

_____

Coverage area (sq. ft.)_____
Purchased from _____

_____

Cost per unit/Total cost_____
Installed by_____
    Date_____
Pattern, color, brand, number_____

_____

Cleaning instructions_____

_____

Notes_____

_____

_____

Walls

Coverage area (sq. ft.)_____

Type of covering_____

_____

Purchased from _____

_____

Cost per unit/Total cost_____

Applied by_____

    Date_____

Pattern, color, brand, number_____

_____

Trim/woodwork_____

_____

Notes_____

_____

_____

Attic

Ceiling

Coverage area (sq. ft.)_____

Type of ceiling_____

Type of covering_____

Purchased from _____
_____

Cost per unit/Total cost_____

Applied by_____

    Date_____

Pattern, color, brand, number_____
_____

Notes_____
_____
_____

Window Treatments

Type of treatments_____
_____

Purchased from _____
_____

Window dimensions (see diagram, page 134)_____
_____
_____

Size of treatments_____
_____

Cleaning instructions_____
_____
_____

Notes_____
_____
_____

Miscellaneous Notes or Layouts

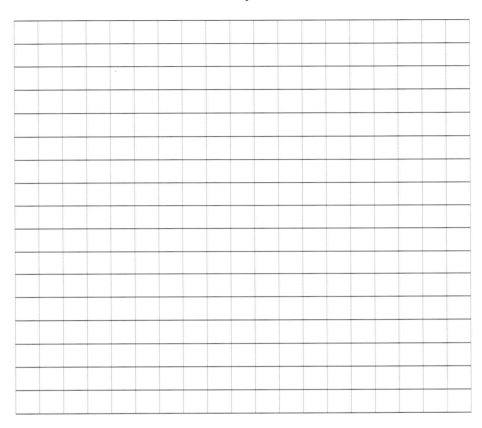

Attach swatches, paint chips, carpet yarns,
or other samples here.

Finished Basement

Room Dimensions _____ x _____ x _____

Goals and priorities for this room_____

_____

_____

_____

_____

_____

_____

_____

_____

_____

_____

Floor

Type of floor (hardwood, tile, concrete, etc.)_____

_____

Type of floor covering_____

_____

Coverage area (sq. ft.)_____

Purchased from _____

_____

Cost per unit/Total cost_____

Installed by_____

    Date_____

Pattern, color, brand, number_____

_____

Cleaning instructions_____

_____

Notes_____

_____

_____

Walls

Coverage area (sq. ft.)_____

Type of covering_____

_____

Purchased from _____

_____

Cost per unit/Total cost_____

Applied by_____

  Date_____

Pattern, color, brand, number_____

_____

Trim/woodwork_____

_____

Notes_____

_____

_____

Finished Basement

Ceiling

Coverage area (sq. ft.)_____

Type of ceiling_____

Type of covering_____

Purchased from _____

_____

Cost per unit/Total cost_____

Applied by_____

　　　Date_____

Pattern, color, brand, number_____

_____

Notes_____

_____

_____

Window Treatments

Type of treatments_____

_____

Purchased from _____

_____

Window dimensions (see diagram, page 134)_____

_____

_____

Size of treatments_____

_____

Cleaning instructions_____

_____

_____

Notes_____

_____

_____

Miscellaneous Notes or Layouts

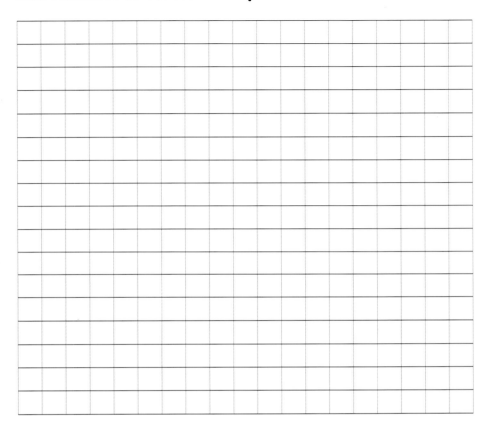

Attach swatches, paint chips, carpet yarns,
or other samples here.

Additional Room:

Room Dimensions _____ x _____ x _____

Goals and priorities for this room _____

_____

_____

_____

_____

_____

_____

_____

_____

_____

Floor

Type of floor (hardwood, tile, concrete, etc.) _____

_____

Type of floor covering _____

_____

Coverage area (sq. ft.) _____

Purchased from _____

_____

Cost per unit/Total cost _____

Installed by _____

　　　Date _____

Pattern, color, brand, number _____

_____

Cleaning instructions _____

_____

Notes _____

_____

_____

Walls

Coverage area (sq. ft.)_____

Type of covering _____

_____

Purchased from _____

_____

Cost per unit/Total cost _____

Applied by_____

    Date_____

Pattern, color, brand, number_____

_____

Trim/woodwork_____

_____

Notes_____

_____

_____

Additional Room:

Ceiling

Coverage area (sq. ft.)_____

Type of ceiling_____

Type of covering_____

Purchased from _____

_____

Cost per unit/Total cost_____

Applied by_____

    Date_____

Pattern, color, brand, number_____

_____

Notes_____

_____

_____

Window Treatments

Type of treatments_____

_____

Purchased from _____

_____

Window dimensions (see diagram, page 134)_____

_____

_____

Size of treatments_____

_____

Cleaning instructions_____

_____

_____

Notes_____

_____

_____

Miscellaneous Notes or Layouts

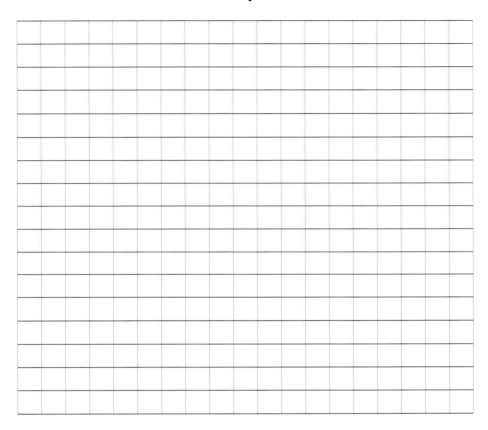

Attach swatches, paint chips, carpet yarns,
or other samples here.

Additional Room:

Room Dimensions _____ x _____ x _____

Goals and priorities for this room_____

_____

_____

_____

_____

_____

_____

_____

_____

_____

Floor

Type of floor (hardwood, tile, concrete, etc.)_____

_____

Type of floor covering_____

_____

Coverage area (sq. ft.)_____

Purchased from_____

_____

Cost per unit/Total cost_____

Installed by_____

    Date_____

Pattern, color, brand, number_____

_____

Cleaning instructions_____

_____

Notes_____

_____

_____

Walls

Coverage area (sq. ft.)_____

Type of covering_____

_____

Purchased from _____

_____

Cost per unit/Total cost_____

Applied by_____

Date_____

Pattern, color, brand, number_____

_____

Trim/woodwork_____

_____

Notes_____

_____

_____

Additional Room:

Ceiling

Coverage area (sq. ft.)_____

Type of ceiling_____

Type of covering_____

Purchased from _____
_____

Cost per unit/Total cost_____

Applied by_____

Date_____

Pattern, color, brand, number_____
_____

Notes_____
_____
_____

Window Treatments

Type of treatments_____
_____

Purchased from _____
_____

Window dimensions (see diagram, page 134)_____
_____
_____

Size of treatments_____
_____

Cleaning instructions_____
_____
_____

Notes_____
_____
_____

Miscellaneous Notes or Layouts

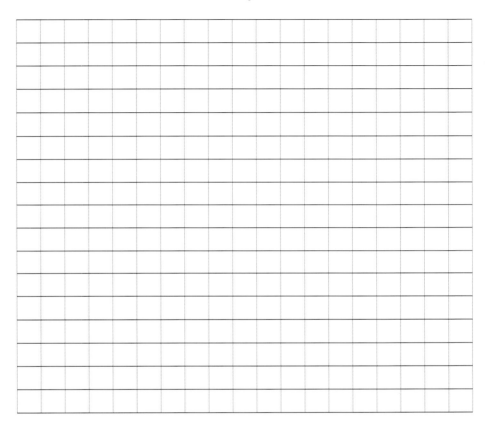

Attach swatches, paint chips, carpet yarns,
or other samples here.

Additional Room:

Room Dimensions _____ x _____ x _____

Goals and priorities for this room _____
_____
_____
_____
_____
_____
_____
_____
_____
_____
_____

Floor

Type of floor (hardwood, tile, concrete, etc.) _____
_____

Type of floor covering _____
_____

Coverage area (sq. ft.) _____
Purchased from _____
_____

Cost per unit/Total cost _____
Installed by _____
    Date _____
Pattern, color, brand, number _____
_____

Cleaning instructions _____
_____

Notes _____
_____
_____

Walls

Coverage area (sq. ft.)_____

Type of covering_____

_____

Purchased from _____

_____

Cost per unit/Total cost_____

Applied by_____

    Date_____

Pattern, color, brand, number_____

_____

Trim/woodwork_____

_____

Notes_____

_____

_____

Additional Room:

Ceiling

Coverage area (sq. ft.)_____

Type of ceiling_____

Type of covering_____

Purchased from_____

_____

Cost per unit/Total cost_____

Applied by_____

Date_____

Pattern, color, brand, number_____

_____

Notes_____

_____

_____

Window Treatments

Type of treatments_____

_____

Purchased from_____

_____

Window dimensions (see diagram, page 134)_____

_____

_____

Size of treatments_____

_____

Cleaning instructions_____

_____

_____

Notes_____

_____

_____

Miscellaneous Notes or Layouts

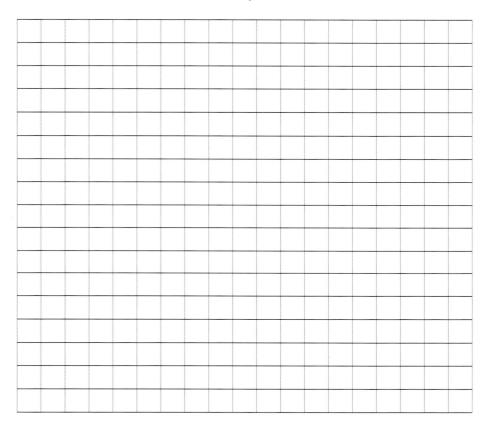

Attach swatches, paint chips, carpet yarns,
or other samples here.

Decorating Ideas

Use the furniture templates below as guides to sketch out room designs on the following grid pages. The pocket on the last page of this book can be used to store decorating or home maintenance ideas found in magazines or books.

Scale: 1/4" = 1'-0"

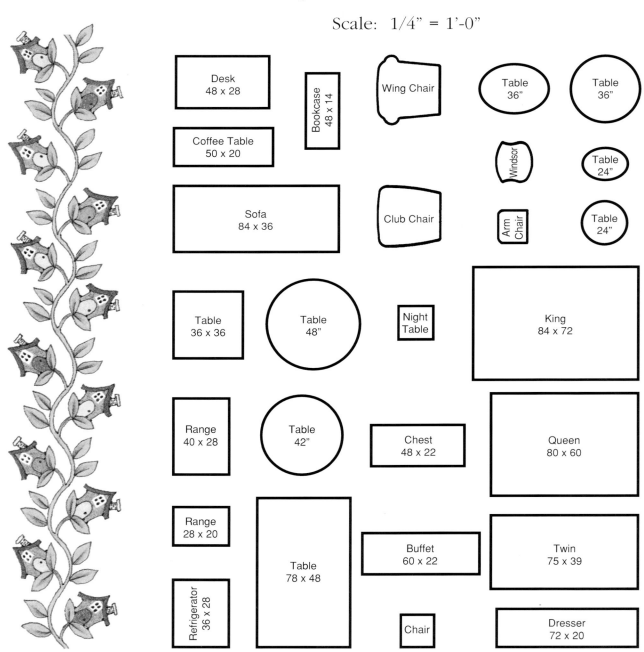

Desk
48 x 28

Bookcase
48 x 14

Wing Chair

Table
36"

Table
36"

Coffee Table
50 x 20

Windsor

Table
24"

Sofa
84 x 36

Club Chair

Arm
Chair

Table
24"

Table
36 x 36

Table
48"

Night
Table

King
84 x 72

Range
40 x 28

Table
42"

Chest
48 x 22

Queen
80 x 60

Range
28 x 20

Table
78 x 48

Buffet
60 x 22

Twin
75 x 39

Refrigerator
36 x 28

Chair

Dresser
72 x 20

Exterior/Outdoor Journal

House Exterior

Roof

Type of roofing_____

_____

Purchased from/Installed by, date_____

_____

Coverage area (sq. ft.)_____

Cost per unit/Total cost_____

Style, brand, color_____

_____

Notes_____

_____

Gutters and Downspouts

Type (Aluminum, steel, copper, box, etc.)_____

_____

Purchased from/Installed by, date_____

_____

Cost per unit/Total cost_____

Style, brand, color_____

_____

Notes_____

_____

Storm Windows and Doors

Purchased from_____

_____

Purchased from/Installed by, date_____

_____

Cost_____

Notes_____

_____

Siding

Type of siding (vinyl, wood, brick, etc.)_____

_____

Purchased from _____

_____

Installed by_____

　　　　Date_____

Coverage area (sq. ft.)_____

Cost per unit/Total cost_____

Style, brand, color_____

_____

Notes_____

_____

Exterior Trim

Type of trim (wood, aluminum, etc.)_____

_____

Type of treatment (paint, stain, etc.)_____

_____

Pattern, color, brand, number_____

_____

Cost per unit/Total cost_____

Applied by_____

　　　　Date_____

Notes_____

_____

Attach paint chips here.

Garage

Roof

Type of roofing_____

_____

Purchased from/Installed by, date_____

_____

Coverage area (sq. ft.)_____

Cost per unit/Total cost_____

Style, brand, color_____

_____

Notes_____

_____

_____

_____

_____

_____

Gutters and Downspouts

Type (Aluminum, steel, copper, box, etc.)_____

_____

Purchased from/Installed by, date_____

_____

Cost per unit/Total cost_____

Style, brand, color_____

_____

Notes_____

_____

_____

_____

_____

_____

Siding

Type of siding (vinyl, wood, brick, etc.)_____

_____

Purchased from _____

_____

Installed by_____

     Date_____

Coverage area (sq. ft.)_____

Cost per unit/Total cost_____

Style, brand, color_____

_____

Notes_____

_____

Trim

Type of trim (wood, aluminum, etc.)_____

_____

Type of treatment (paint, stain, etc.)_____

_____

Pattern, color, brand, number_____

_____

Cost per unit/Total cost_____

Applied by_____

     Date_____

Notes_____

_____

Attach paint chips here.

Outdoor Areas & Structures

Deck

Materials, date built, built by whom, finish, maintenance, etc.

_____

_____

_____

_____

_____

_____

_____

Patio

Materials, date installed, installed by whom, finish, maintenance, etc.

_____

_____

_____

_____

_____

_____

_____

Porch

Materials, date built, built by whom, finish, maintenance, etc.

_____

_____

_____

_____

_____

_____

Driveway

Materials, date installed, installed by whom, finish, maintenance, etc.

_____

_____

_____

_____

Fence

Materials, date built, built by whom, finish, maintenance, etc.

_____

_____

_____

_____

_____

_____

Outbuildings

Materials, date built, built by whom, finish, maintenance, etc.

_____

_____

_____

_____

_____

Pool

Materials, date built, built by whom, finish, maintenance, etc.

_____

_____

_____

_____

_____

Miscellaneous Records
and
Reference

Heating & Cooling System Records

Air Conditioner

Purchased from _____

Date _____

Cost _____

Brand name, model number _____

Warranty information _____

Service phone number _____

Notes _____

Furnace

Purchased from _____

Date _____

Cost _____

Brand name, model number _____

Warranty information _____

Service phone number _____

Notes _____

Heat Pump

Purchased from _____

Date _____

Cost _____

Brand name, model number _____

Heat Pump (continued)

Warranty information _____

_____

Service phone number _____

Notes _____

_____

Wood Stove

Purchased from _____

      Date _____

Cost _____

Brand name, model number _____

_____

Warranty information _____

_____

Service phone number _____

Notes _____

_____

Fireplace

Purchased from _____

      Date _____

Cost _____

Brand name, model number _____

_____

Warranty information _____

_____

Service phone number _____

Notes _____

_____

_____

Appliances & Accessories

Refrigerator

Purchased from _____

     Date _____

Cost _____

Brand name, model number _____

_____

Warranty information _____

Service phone number _____

Notes _____

Dishwasher

Purchased from _____

     Date _____

Cost _____

Brand name, model number _____

_____

Warranty information _____

Service phone number _____

Notes _____

Stove/Oven

Purchased from _____

     Date _____

Cost _____

Brand name, model number _____

_____

Warranty information _____

Service phone number _____

Notes _____

_____

_____

Cooktop

Purchased from _____

     Date _____

Cost _____

Brand name, model number _____

_____

Warranty information _____

Service phone number _____

Notes _____

Microwave Oven

Purchased from _____

     Date _____

Cost _____

Brand name, model number _____

_____

Warranty information _____

Service phone number _____

Notes _____

Miscellaneous Appliance

Purchased from _____

     Date _____

Cost _____

Brand name, model number _____

_____

Warranty information _____

Service phone number _____

Notes _____

_____

_____

Appliances & Accessories

Washing Machine

Purchased from _____

      Date _____

Cost _____

Brand name, model number _____

_____

Warranty information _____

Service phone number _____

Notes _____

Clothes Dryer

Purchased from _____

      Date _____

Cost _____

Brand name, model number _____

_____

Warranty information _____

Service phone number _____

Notes _____

Electronic Garage Door Opener

Purchased from _____

      Date _____

Cost _____

Brand name, model number _____

_____

Warranty information _____

Service phone number _____

Notes _____

_____

_____

Alarm/Security System

Purchased from _____

    Date _____

Cost _____

Brand name, model number _____

_____

Warranty information _____

Service phone number _____

Notes _____

Smoke Detectors

Purchased from _____

    Date _____

Cost _____

Brand name, model number _____

_____

Warranty information _____

Service phone number _____

Notes _____

Miscellaneous Appliance

Purchased from _____

    Date _____

Cost _____

Brand name, model number _____

_____

Warranty information _____

Service phone number _____

Notes _____

_____

_____

Reference

Window Measurements

When measuring windows, note the exact dimensions to the nearest 1/8". In most cases the manufacturer or decorator will make the appropriate adjustments for fit based on the type of window treatment you choose.

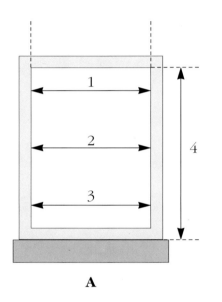

A

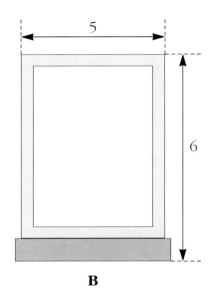

B

A. Inside Frame Mount:
Measure the width of the top (1), middle (2), and bottom (3) and use the narrowest of these measurements.

Measure the length from top inside casing to top of the sill (4).

B. Outside Frame Mount:
Measure the window width outside the casing (5).

Measure the length from top outside casing to bottom of the sill (6).

Ordering Wallcovering

To determine the amount of wallcovering you need, use the simple chart below. Standard metric rolls contain approximately 28.2 square feet regardless of their different widths and lengths. To allow for trimming and matching, plan on 22 square feet of coverage per single metric roll.

Distance around room in feet	Height of Walls				Rolls needed for ceiling
	8 ft. high	9 ft. high	10 ft. high	12 ft. high	
36	12	16	16	20	4
40	16	16	18	20	4
44	16	18	20	24	4
48	16	18	20	26	6
52	18	20	22	28	6
56	20	22	26	30	8
60	20	22	26	30	8
64	22	26	28	34	10
68	22	28	30	36	10
72	26	28	30	38	12

Deduct one single roll, approximately 22 square feet, for each two openings (windows and doors) of ordinary size.

Basic Surface Preparation for Wallcovering

Remove old wallcovering and fill holes/cracks. Use sandpaper on irregular surfaces.
1. Unpainted walls: New plaster must be aged and thoroughly dry. Prime and size.
2. Wallboard: Seal bare surfaces with suitable primer and size.
3. Painted walls: Wash surfaces with household detergent to remove grease, grime, and dust.

Reference

Choosing the Proper House Paint

Type	Characteristics & Uses
Latex	The most popular paint for both interior and exterior. Available in flat, gloss, and semigloss. Very quick drying and odorless. Not for use on unprimed wood, metal, or wallpaper. Covers and blends extremely well. Easy clean-up with soap and water. Water-based and naturally mildew-proof.
Alkyd	Interior and exterior enamels made from synthetic resin. Easy to apply, fast drying, nearly odorless. Produces very tough coating with excellent hiding power. Easy clean-up with mineral spirits (paint thinner). Use it to paint over old oil- or alkyd-based coatings.
Oil Base	As an exterior finish, popularity has greatly diminished. Interior oil base paints have largely disappeared. Extremely slow drying time (12-48 hours). Gives off strong, flammable fumes. Messy clean-up with turpentine or other mineral spirits.
Acrylic	A type of latex. Water-thinned and very quick drying. Will cover almost any material including masonry.

Applying Paint

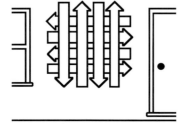

When painting flat surfaces, apply the paint first in long, horizontal strokes. Then cross the horizontal strokes by working up and down (see diagram at left). This will give a completely covered surface and use less paint.

To avoid brush marks, always end the painting of an area by brushing back toward the area already painted.